All Cats Have Asperger Syndrome

also by Kathy Hoopmann

Haze
ISBN 1 84310 072 X

Asperger Adventures

Lisa and the Lacemaker
ISBN 1 84310 071 1

Of Mice and Aliens
ISBN 1 84310 007 X

Blue Bottle Mystery
ISBN 1 85302 978 5

All Cats Have Asperger Syndrome

Kathy Hoopmann

Jessica Kingsley Publishers
London and Philadelphia

First published in 2006
by Jessica Kingsley Publishers
116 Pentonville Road
London N1 9JB, UK
and
400 Market Street, Suite 400
Philadelphia, PA 19106, USA

www.jkp.com

Library of Congress Cataloging in Publication Data

Hoopmann, Kathy, 1963-
All cats have Asperger Syndrome / Kathy Hoopmann.
   p. cm.
ISBN-13: 978-1-84310-481-0 (pbk. : alk. paper)
ISBN-10: 1-84310-481-4 (pbk. : alk. paper) 1. Asperger's syndrome--Juvenile literature. I. Title.
RJ506.A9H65 2007
618.92'858832--dc22
                              2006013021

British Library Cataloguing in Publication Data
A CIP catalogue record for this book is available from the British Library

ISBN-13: 978 1 84310 481 0
ISBN-10: 1 84310 481 4

Printed and bound by Amity Printing
in The People's Republic of China
APC-FT 4501

For Alexandria Bridges
A true lover of cats

The first signs of Asperger Syndrome
are usually picked up very young.

An Asperger child looks at the world in his own unique way.

He likes to be near those he loves,

but doesn't want them to hold him,

preferring
squishy
places
to a hug.

Instead of coming to people for comfort,
          he may be overly attached to a toy...

...or a pet.

It's possible he is extra adventurous
with no sense of danger,

and he uses
up some of his
nine lives all
too quickly.

An Asperger child often has exceptionally
good hearing,

and loud sounds and sudden movements
may scare him.

"These clothes are scratchy!"

His other senses can be heightened too, such as touch

"Phew! It's garbage day again!"

and smell.

"I'm not cold."

Yet things that bother other people may not bother him.

He's often fussy about what he eats...

...and wants
the same food
presented in
the same way,
day after day.

He isn't interested in the things
other kids his age do

and when he's
forced to mix,
he doesn't
know how.

Other kids make friends...

...but don't invite him to play,

and he may be bullied.

Sometimes his parents feel sad,
wondering why they can't understand
their own child,

and they can become very protective.

The Asperger child may feel sad too,

and he
may
become a
loner
caught up
in a world
of his own,

where small things fascinate him for hours

and he
can do
the same
thing over
and over
again...

...without getting bored.

When things
get too much
for him, he
may tantrum.

"In our day...!"

Sometimes his relatives
   think they could bring him up
      better than his parents can.

His vocabulary may be very advanced,

"That was catastrophic, Mum!"

"That doesn't look like a mouse."

but then he gets little words all mixed up

"I haven't let the cat out of the bag."

or misunderstands what people say.

When people talk to him
        he may refuse to look at them.

Yet when HE
talks, he goes
on and on about
the same topic...

"I like black mice and brown mice
and white mice..."

...and bores everyone silly.

"Did you know that a mouse and a man share 97.5% of the same DNA?"

Then he says something
   that makes them stop and think...

...and they marvel at his bright, intelligent mind.

EAT

in many ways his thinking
is far ahead of his peers

"It's all in the balance."

and he seeks
answers in places
others don't think
to look,

or invents
new ways
to do
old things.

"If you wash this way you don't get fur balls."

"If a space is smaller than the width of whiskers, you can't get through."

People may be astounded by how far he is prepared to go to test his latest theory,

and some will
say he's a
little genius.

"Three stretches before each nap."

Daily rituals comfort him,

and he likes a good routine...

"A catnap after breakfast, a catnap after lunch.."

"Mum is 3.26 minutes late!"

...and gets
worried
if the
schedule
is changed.

"Look at that fat man with the big nose!"

**Often an Asperger child has a great
sense of humour, but he doesn't always
think about what he is saying**

and those around him
  may cringe with embarrassment.

"Your face is all crinkly when you're mad, Mum!"

And he is honest,
which is great of course,
but sometimes
he's too honest.

"Bird? What bird?"

Yet when
he tries to
tell a lie,
he's not
very good
at it.

An Asperger child may be very open
　　　　　to all people, regardless of age,

or size,

or species,

**and he may choose friends others
            wouldn't have thought he would like.**

But as he grows older
        he senses that he is different
                from everyone else...

...and feels as if he belongs on a different planet,

like an outsider looking into a world
       he never truly understands.

Yet with his
unique
perspective
on life,

his eye
for detail,

and his amazing powers of concentration,

many an Asperger child has reached the top of his chosen field.

Business tycoon

Judge

CAT

Professor

Sure, he may need a little help following fashionable trends,

but don't forget,
everyone is different
in his own way and there is
 a little bit of Asperger in us all.

So an Asperger child is just like any other child.

He needs love and encouragement,

the occasional bit of advice,

space to be himself,

and then everyone can sit back and enjoy the unique individual he becomes.